The Day They Hung The Elephant

Charles Edwin Price

Illustrations by Randy Hodge

The Overmountain Press

JOHNSON CITY, TENNESSEE

ISBN 0-932807-75-5
Printed in the United States of America

2 3 4 5 6 7 8 9 0

For
Richard Blaustein
With Gratitude

Foreword

Our first apartment on North Roan Street was kerosene heated, linoleum-floored, and boasted four rooms. It was almost on the curb and its view was of an elementary school, massive trucks and two gas stations. This was 1959 and the Johnson City *Press-Chronicle* cost 60-cents a week, including Sundays. I read it avidly and with many questions—having come from large cities with two or three dailies, and lots of national news about places everyone knew about.

Now I tried to learn about Flag Pond, Bulls Gap, Fordtown, Piney Flats, Embreeville and Happy Valley. I was especially intrigued by the byline "Unicoi". The news about this place involved apple and ramp festivals. I finally asked my Texaco man, very seriously, "What is Unicoi?" "Oh, it's a town and a county over south of here. That's where Erwin is." "Who's Erwin?" "It's a railroad town. They hung an elephant there once." I was sure Roy was pulling a trick on a naive Yankee—but he was usually a pretty serious guy. He told me about the elephant—and I later saw the famous news photo. I became a believer.

Now it's interesting to tell newcomers about the elephant—they often think it's a tall tale.

Like all local tales, told by numerous people with second, third, and sixth hand knowledge, the elephant story has acquired quite an array of lore and legend along with fact. Ed Price has gone through the sources, analyzed the material, sorted fact from fantasy, to produce the story of "Murderous Mary", the elephant hanged for murder in 1916. His narrative, based on many hours of research, is lively, full of suspense, vivid in detail—a proof once again that fact can be as enthralling as fiction. Sometimes, more so.

The story of Mary is one that can be told and retold, read and reread, with no loss of excitement. To have it in finished narrative form is to insure that it will not fade away. The enigmas will be there to be argued over; there will be room for speculation, still. More than one kibitzer will declare that his grandfather, or her great-great uncle was alive when the hanging took place—maybe even witnessed it. Ed's narrative, however, will serve as a definitive work on what was possibly the last public lynching of a large animal for reasons other than witch hunting.

Anne LeCroy
East Tennessee State University
Spring 1992

Preface

There is no doubt that, in 1916, a five-ton circus elephant was lynched from a 100-ton Clinchfield Railroad crane car in the little town of Erwin, Tennessee. The details of the execution and the tragic events leading up to it, however, are clouded in nearly a century of oral tradition. From one retelling to the next, facts are distorted and embellished; legend, instead of truth, is often accepted as fact. This book is an attempt to bring together all the known facts about the hanging, and to fill in with educated guesses the missing parts of the puzzle. This is a story filled with enigmas.

I do not believe that my version of the story of Mary, however, is complete. No retelling could ever be. Official records of the event are sparse. Reliable circus records are almost nonexistent, and those that are extant leave a lot of room for interpretation. Even contemporary newspaper reports of the hanging differ widely in most details. Most of my telling of the story has, of necessity, been pieced together based on eyewitness accounts which I have checked against the facts. With so many loose ends dangling, I often have been tempted to distort the facts myself for the sake óf drama. Fortunately, for the sake of my own credibility, I have kept my imagination in check. *The facts that have emerged*, I found, were more intriguing than anything I could have contrived in a flight of fancy.

The bizarre story of the hanging of Mary the elephant begins in St. Paul, Virginia, where Sparks World Famous Shows stopped for a one-day stand. The story ends in Erwin, three days later. Between these little towns ran the shiny twin rails of the Carolina, Clinchfield and Ohio Railroad (popularly known as "The Clinchfield"). Like the blazing skyscraper in the film *The Towering Inferno*, the Clinchfield is an indispensable prop in the story of Mary and those people whose lives she touched.

The Clinchfield, like most American railroads, hauled freight cars as a service for traveling circuses. Since most shows owned their own rolling stock, all the host railway provided was engine and track. Located on the Clinchfield's main line, St. Paul (Virginia), Kingsport, Johnson City and Erwin were frequent stopping-off places for traveling shows. In addition, the Clinchfield was the primary coal carrier in the area, an economic power in upper East Tennessee and Southwest Virginia. Industry and mining depended on the Clinchfield to transport goods to market. In return the railroad involved itself in the political and social life of the towns it touched. On one occasion the Clinchfield provided support over and above the call of duty. Without the Clinchfield's able assistance, Erwin could not have attained the dubious fame as the place where they hanged the elephant.

Charles Edwin Price
Johnson City, Tennessee
May 1992

Acknowledgments

The Archives of Appalachia contains one of the richest repositories of folklore research, books and historical papers in Eastern Tennessee. Located in the Sherrod Library at East Tennessee State University, it was here that most of my research for this book was done. The Archives is home to the complete Clinchfield Railroad records, maps and charts, donated when the Clinchfield was absorbed by CSX in the 1970s. There is also a library of regional publications, clippings from newspapers, old photographs, letters and manuscripts that are valuable to researchers.

Here, too, lies the vast body of audio and video tapes, and papers, collected in the 1960s by ETSU professors Thomas Burton and Ambrose Manning. Included in this collection are recollections from a number of people who were eyewitnesses to the hanging of Mary.

Poring over this wealth of material was a never-ending challenge for one person. But Norma Myers, Marie Tedesco, Georgia Greer, Ed Speer and Scott Schwartz made my task much easier with their unerring ability to instantly locate the appropriate materials at the appropriate moment. To these dedicated archivists goes my undying gratitude.

Thanks, too, to Joe Snyder, proprietor of the Clinchfield Drug Store in Erwin. Each morning about 9 a.m., the "old salts" of Erwin gather at his lunch counter to gossip and swap stories. Just listening to them was an experience. Joe helped me locate eyewitnesses to Mary's hanging.

Erwinite Guard Banner and his son, Bob, spent much time with me during my research. Guard told me about his recollections of the hanging and made certain that I *completely understood* the method by which Mary was hung. Guard is a folklorist's dream. Although in his nineties, his memory is sharp, and he loves to recount past experiences. I would also like to express my deep appreciation to Angie Edwards, my good friend at ETSU, for introducing me to Guard (her great-grandfather) in the first place.

Thanks, too, to those wonderful, trusting Erwinites who provided treasured photographs for the book. And *a very special thanks* to Eddie LeSueur, longtime photographer for the Johnson City *Press*, for the extra effort he put forth in making new prints of the famous photo of Mary hanging from the gallows, as well as his invaluable information on the background of the picture.

Last, but certainly not least, I want to thank two special women who have offered me more help and encouragement than any one person deserves—Linda Carmichel and Anne LeCroy. Thank you for reading my manuscript, for your patience, your valuable suggestions and criticisms. Linda is one of those rare people with the uncanny ability to combine scholarship and popular writing style, and to point out to this writer (in no uncertain terms) when his writing becomes stuffy and self-important. Anne, on the other hand, has a sure cure for writer's "block-n-gloom"—her homemade gingerbread. Anne also insists—quite correctly—that scholarly writing doesn't have to be stuffy. Without Anne's and Linda's input, this book would never have reached its final form.

I would also like to thank Anne LeCroy for her kindness in writing the Foreword to this book.

Monday, September 11, 1916

Shortly before 6 a.m. Walter "Red" Eldridge, general handyman, janitor, and porter for the Riverside Hotel, strode briskly down the main thoroughfare of St. Paul, Virginia. The sun was just nosing over the mountains beyond the winding Clinch River, and St. Paul streets were beginning to show signs of life. A mining community, St. Paul began its day early.

Red Eldridge was an outsider in St. Paul. People in most small, rural Southern communities ordinarily kept to themselves. Outsiders, especially drifters, were regarded with suspicion. St. Paul took care of its own.

Eldridge hated his job at the Riverside Hotel, but he hated hunger even more. He had recently drifted into St. Paul via the Norfolk and Western Railroad and was flirting with starvation when he found a job at the Riverside. At $1.50 a week, Eldrige considered himself a rich man, but a week later the drifter in his soul took over, and Eldridge longed for greener pastures.

A block from the Riverside Hotel, Eldridge quickened his pace. When he entered the lobby, he glanced uneasily at the big Regulator clock hanging on the wall behind the check-in desk. "I see you have your wits about you this morning," a gruff-looking man growled from behind the wooden front desk. "For once you're on time."

"Yes sir," Eldridge answered quickly, slightly out of breath. His thin frame, predominant adam's apple, long thin neck and red hair made him look a bit like an outsized turkey gobbler.

Without ceremony, the hotel's manager thrust a ragged broom into Eldridge's hand. "The porch needs swept," he said brusquely.

Eldridge heaved the broom over his shoulder and ambled through the heavy double wooden doors onto the plank front porch. As he swept, his broom raised little puffs of brown dust. Clay and mud from the street caked in hard red and gray clods on the wood's surface. Eldridge broke the clods by poking them with the rounded end of his broom handle, then he swept the dust into the street. He had worked only five minutes when he noticed two men—strangers like himself in St. Paul—walking briskly down the street.

Each man stopped at a tree or light pole, tacked up a gaily-colored poster and moved on. Eldridge strolled to the nearest tree and read one of the bills. A smile spread across his ruddy, freckled face. Sparks World Famous Shows was coming to St. Paul.

At least once each summer, the attention of small town America switched from mundane agrarianism to worldly glitz—an escape signaled by the arrival of the circus train. The large traveling shows, like John Robinson's Four Ring Circus and Menagerie, usually passed St. Paul for big towns like Johnson City, 30 miles to the south. Sparks World Famous Shows, modest by contemporary standards, found it profitable to stop in small towns like St. Paul.

Eldridge's imagination soared. As a boy in Indiana he was often waiting at the siding when the circus train chugged into town. His friends were there too, hoping for a job—back-breaking work rewarded with free tickets to the show. Competition was keen because some circus jobs carried higher status than others. For instance, shoveling manure was not as important a job as carrying water to the livestock. A job shoveling horse dung was believed beneath the dignity of even the most avid circus buff. Luckily, no one ever thrust a pitchfork into young Red's hand—it had always been a water bucket.

There was a dangerous side in carrying water to the livestock, especially to elephants. Eldridge was probably lectured a hundred times by animal trainers not to trust an elephant—pour your water in the trough and stay out of reach of the long trunk. An elephant with a curious trunk was an elephant who might suddenly wrap the appendage around you, lift you up and dash you to the ground. Elephants, a hundred times stronger than the strongest man, go berserk and think nothing of crushing the nearest human like an ant.

Male elephants are more unpredictable than females because of a manifestation called musth. Once a year, glands in the male's skull secrete an evil-smelling tarlike substance. During musth, males are chained for their own protection and the protection of humans around them. Females, on the other hand, rarely suffer from musth. Showmen learned this biological fact early, but not before a brace of keepers had been killed or seriously injured by rampaging pachyderms. Eventually, females replaced males as the dominant sex in captivity. They were more docile and predictable—most of the time.

Female elephants, too, were known to throw "hissy fits" but, in most cases, there were extenuating circumstances. An elephant named Dolly, for instance, ran amok in Chicago during the Exposition. She destroyed a lot of property until finally quelled by her trainer. Thankfully, no one was injured.

What was the reason for Dolly's behavior? Someone had brought a small white dog to the Exposition, and the animal began yapping at Dolly's heels. Dolly could have crushed the noisy creature with one of her giant feet. Instead, she panicked, ran through the crowded Exposition, and endangered everyone in her mad rush to escape the tiny animal.

Red Eldridge gazed at the handbill hastily tacked on an elm tree. An elephant named "Mary" stared back at him from the poster. Eldridge read the print underneath the drawing:

Mary. The Largest Living Land Animal On Earth.
3 Inches Taller Than Jumbo and Weighing Over 5 Tons.

In the same drawing was the figure of a man—a normal size person. According to the drawing's scale, Mary the elephant looked 30 feet tall! Impossible! Then Eldridge spied a footnote printed at the lower left-hand corner of the poster: "A grand free street parade—each day at noon."

"Wonderful," he thought to himself. "I'll watch the parade, go see the show, and then visit the circus boss. Maybe I can get a job as an animal trainer and leave this town."

As Eldridge walked back across the street toward the Riverside Hotel, his mind reeled with visions of glory. A golden opportunity presented itself. He was footloose and fancy-free—no attachments to keep him in St. Paul. He had always wanted to join the circus. It was now or never.

The big top canvas was nearly pulled to the top of the tall center poles as Charlie Sparks, the circus owner, began his traditional early-morning stroll over the grounds. Sparks was a careful showman—one who sought both profit and quality. Everything must be just right for the "rubes" (customers). If not, heads would roll.

Charlie Sparks began his career in the 1890s with a dog and pony show. His father, John H. Sparks, formed Sparks World Famous Shows the same year. He combined his show with that of his son; Charlie's animals were billed as an "Equine and Canine Paradox." When the elder Sparks died a few years later, Charlie inherited the whole shebang. He expanded the menagerie to include elephants, lions, a giraffe and seals.

Although small, Charlie's show boasted quality. But no matter how hard he tried, Charlie Sparks was unable to raise his show beyond the one-horse variety. There was just too much competition from bigger traveling shows, and Charlie couldn't raise enough capital for real expansion.

In the days of traveling railroad shows, the size and importance of a circus was determined by how much rolling stock it owned, as well as the number of elephants in its menagerie. John Robinson's Four Ring Circus and Menagerie, Sparks' major competitor in the South, boasted 42 railroad cars. According to their lavish advertising, Robinson's show featured, in addition to almost a dozen elephants, 22 tents, eight separate bands, 95 acrobats, 82 aerialists, 60 horses, 50 "noted circus stars," 50 animal trainers, and 51 clowns—a total of 387 performers.

No one knows for sure how many performers Sparks World Famous Shows had. Their equally lavish advertising claimed 20 clowns and an elephant herd of five, including Mary. Their rail transportation consisted of one executive car, two box cars and seven flat cars.

Although Sparks' circus was considered small when compared to Robinson's, it was much larger than some of the other traveling shows of the day. Frank Adams claimed only two cars; the Don Carlos Dog, Pony, and Monkey Show, a like number. Mollie Bailey had three.

Along with the small circuses riding the rails, there were also monster shows in competition with them. The largest of all, Barnum and Bailey, had 84 cars; Forepaugh-Sells had 47. The Buffalo Bill-Pawneee Bill Wild West Show traveled in 59 cars. And the Miller Brothers and Edward Arlington's 101 Ranch Wild West (which featured a then unknown western trick rider named Tom Mix) traveled in 27 cars.

Charlie Sparks stopped long enough on his morning walk to watch Henri Mordette practice his act. Mordette was Sparks' star performer. Billed as "The Man Who Walks Upon His Head," Mordette worked with a four-foot-long platform with two pairs of steps leading up each side. He began his act by standing on his head at the foot of one set of steps, then he ascended the stairs on his head. He bounced along the platform, then descended the other set of steps in the same way. As the finale, Mordette fastened a roller skate to his head and, after getting a good head start down a ramp, jumped a four-foot gap.

A little farther along on his walk, Sparks passed Jim Woodward's collection of snow white "posing" dogs and horses. For his act Woodward whitened his dogs and horses with powder. Several humans, their bodies smeared liberally with clown-white greasepaint, took on the color of marble. The ensemble struck various dramatic poses during their act, attempting to emulate Greek statues.

The barking of seals directed Sparks' attention to another crowd-pleaser, Captain Tiebor and his "educated sea lions." Tiebor and his sea lions were an expensive attraction for Sparks. They were fed with *live, raw saltwater fish,* and it cost the circus about $10 a day to board them. Furthermore, the seals were doused almost constantly with water to prevent their delicate skins from drying out. But they were amiable creatures, natural clowns, and a valuable asset to the show. Their comic presence alone sold hundreds of tickets for each performance.

During his morning walk Charlie Sparks met John Heron, his long-time publicist. "Are we ready for St. Paul?" Sparks asked.

Heron was a little man, filled with nervous energy. "Everything is out," Heron replied quickly. "The parade is scheduled to start at 10 o'clock."

Sparks nodded approval and Heron went his way. Sparks depended on Heron to make sure the tour ran smoothly. Heron's advance men were already in Kingsport, Tennessee, placing posters for the next day's performance. The day after that the circus was scheduled to stop in Erwin, the next day in Johnson City. The show would then move to a one-day stand in Rogersville.

Sparks knew he was fortunate to have shows booked so close together, especially since John Robinson's tour was close on his heels, scheduled to play Johnson City on September 26. Unfortunately Johnson City might prove a sticky problem for Sparks World Famous Shows since the city commission had recently passed an ordinance restricting carnivals.

A carnival (or fair) differed from a circus in that a carnival had no big top and few acrobats—their major income derived from games of chance. A carnival consisted of a very long midway lined with game booths. More than likely, the booths were operated by shady operators—often hired especially for the occasion. For this reason carnivals were held in low esteem by municipalities and were less welcome in a town than circuses. Sometimes traveling carnivals disguised themselves as circuses by adding a small menagerie or sideshow, but wholesale fleecing of rubes continued unabated.

At the September 5, 1916, council meeting, Johnson City Mayor S. E. Miller encouraged the City Council to pass an ordinance extracting a heavy privilege tax from carnivals and fairs—a tax so stiff that it would discourage shady operations from stopping off in town. The Council appointed a committee of three citizens to inspect all visiting shows, to decide for themselves which were bona fide circuses and which were actually carnivals in disguise.

By way of definition, Sparks had little to worry about. His was clearly a circus. Still, the connotation was clear. Johnson City was looking for an excuse to ban any traveling show from town. If Charlie Sparks wanted to be welcome in Johnson City again, he would have to watch his p's and q's.

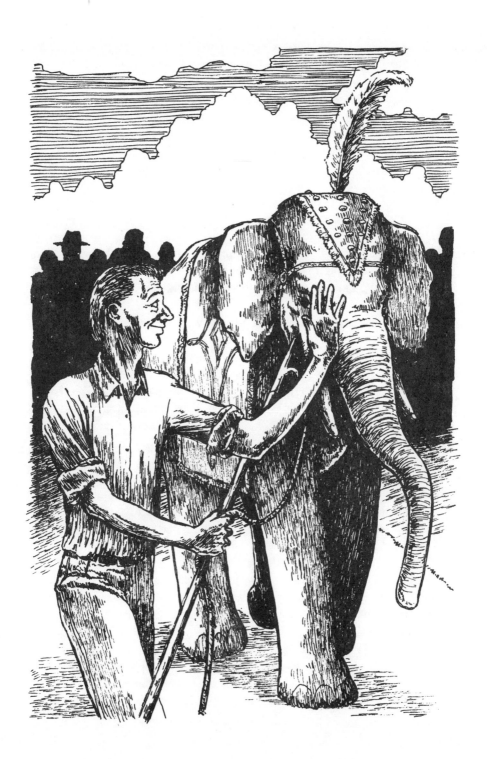

The colorful gala circus parade made its way down St. Paul's main street about noon. Nearly everyone employed by Sparks World Famous Shows participated in the parade; nearly every menagerie animal marched along to the pounding rhythm of an enthusiastic 14-piece, slightly out of tune, brass band.

Brightly colored red and blue tableau wagons pulled by richly decorated horses led the way. These were huge vehicles, so tall that they were dangerously top-heavy. A slight miscalculation when turning a corner could send the wagon toppling to the ground.

Next came a smaller flatbed wagon bearing the cages of Sparks' pair of ragged lions—one male, the other a female. Captain Tiebor's seals occupied a second flatbed wagon, festooned with red and yellow bunting. The animals were joyfully barking and clapping their long black flippers.

Sprinkled liberally throughout the parade were clowns in their colorful makeup and gaudy, outsized costumes. Often they broke away from the procession and mixed with the crowd of onlookers lining both sides of the street. There they greeted hordes of delighted children and adults, shaking their hands vigorously, displaying wide greasepaint smiles, and urging attendance at the upcoming show.

Then came the elephants. Red Eldridge, too, was in the parade. He had not waited until after the matinee to approach the head animal trainer. About an hour after seeing the poster, he handed in his broom to the manager of the Riverside Hotel, collected his pay, and walked to the circus grounds. Luck was with him—an extra trainer was needed. The boss put an elephant stick in his hand and told him to help loose and dress the elephants for the parade.

Eldridge helped unpack the large red blankets trimmed with silver and gold braid that the elephants wore on their backs in parades and during the show. Then he was put in charge of Mabel, a half-grown Indian elephant. With some difficulty he managed to place the red and yellow halter around Mabel's head, making certain that the bright blue imitation feather was positioned correctly in the center. Then he stood back and admired his handiwork. Mabel snorted approval.

All during the parade Eldridge walked proudly at Mabel's side, waving happily to the crowd lining the streets and smiling broadly. He was clearly enjoying himself and feeling important. At parade's end, the keeper told Eldridge to disassemble Mabel's parade wardrobe, water her and give her some hay.

Although Eldridge did not participate in the elephant act during the actual circus performance (he was unfamiliar with the routine), he nevertheless stood on the sidelines, elephant stick in hand. He was told to smear some clown-white greasepaint on his face, and one of the regular clowns reddened his lips. Then the clown outlined Eldridge's eyes with black, put a red ball over his nose, and loaned Eldridge a wild fright wig that was nearly as red as his own natural hair.

Eldridge noticed that he was *not the only one made up so.* Six or seven others, workers like himself, also wore a layer of clown-white. There were only 18 or 20 regular clowns employed by the circus. Now Eldridge *knew why* there were always so many clowns in a circus. Some were not even clowns at all.

The tent was nearly full for both performances in St. Paul. About halfway through the show the elephants marched into the ring, attended by three expert trainers. Mary led the way because she was the largest. The other four in the herd followed, the trunk of the one behind entwined in the tail of the one in front (trunk-to-tail, as it was called). Since she was the smallest, Mabel brought up the rear. The crowd roared in anticipation.

Tricks the elephants performed were typical of the period. First the elephants sat on their haunches, their trunks high in the air, and trumpeted loudly. Then, prodded by the trainers, they stood on their heads. Then each elephant put its forelegs on the back of the one in front of it, forming an elephantine train. As each of these tricks was performed, the crowd roared its approval.

After the evening performance the circus packed up its tents and equipment for the overnight journey to Kingsport. Again Eldridge was put in charge of Mabel, who helped with the loading of the circus onto the train in spite of her size. When all were on board, a Clinchfield steam engine, smokestack belching thick clouds of gray and white smoke, backed up to the siding and coupled onto the train. With a blast of the whistle, a rush of steam, and the clank of metal couplings jerking and grinding against each other, Sparks' rolling stock moved slowly forward, then southward toward the circus's next stop in Kingsport and Red Eldridge's date with destiny.

Tuesday, September 12, 1916

On the overnight trip between St. Paul and Kingsport, Red Eldridge rode with the elephants. Accompanying him was another trainer who had been with Sparks about three months. The trainer offered Eldridge a bunk in the little compartment in the front of the car, but Eldridge was too excited to sleep. Instead he stayed with Mary, Mabel, Shadrack, and the rest of the herd.

All through the night, in the swaying boxcar, Eldridge kept vigil on his animals, talking softly to them. He had grown fond of little Mabel— she was his favorite. And she apparently liked him. Every once in a while she would nuzzle against him like a puppy, demanding affection. Then he would scratch her on the trunk and say a few words.

Mary was another matter. Tethered on the far side of the car, she seemed aloof. Eldridge feared her, but he could not let that show. He wanted her to trust him. While Eldrige felt fondness for Mabel, he was in awe of Mary. To have Mary obey him, perhaps even to show affection, was a challenge to Eldridge. But there was something about her that Eldridge didn't trust—something about her (maybe her sheer bulk) that made him uneasy.

Kingsport, Tennessee, was in the midst of an economic boom, and the town was as bustling as any cattle town in the old west. Unlike St. Paul, which was suffering an economic slump because of the mechanization of the coal fields, Kingsport was a boom town—rip-roaring and busting loose at the seams.

The open fields between Main and Center Streets were dotted with white canvas tents, temporary shelters for new workers and their families that were continually streaming into town. Two hundred homes were in various stages of completion. Business lots sold for as little as $187.50. Hogs freely roamed the town as scavengers. Streets were muddy and sidewalks practically nonexistent. Wagons, horses and people slogged through the gummy roadways. Seeing Kingsport, one would find it hard to imagine there was method to the madness—but there was. The name of the madness was "industry."

In 1900 financier George L. Carter quietly optioned 7,000 acres of land along the Holston River at $30 an acre. Included in his option was the little town of Kingsport. The town originally consisted of a dock and boat yard on the Holston River. It had been settled by William King in 1802 for the purpose of shipping salt.

Since that time, the town had grown little. The nearby towns of Christianville and Rossville were also included in Carter's land deal. His plan was to build the new industrial city of Kingsport. When land-owners eventually discovered that Carter planned to build his Clinchfield Railroad through the center of the property, thereby increasing the land value a hundredfold, some yelled "foul." Outraged landowners held out for a higher settlement price. Eventually Carter settled to everyone's satisfaction. He named his purchase Kingsport Farms and hired Mr. and Mrs. J. W. Dobbins to manage the property.

Carter needed more financing to build his industrial city and complete his railroad. He hired The Blair Company, one of Wall Street's largest municipal bond companies, to help. One of Blair's most trusted associates, John B. Dennis, traveled to Kingsport to oversee the project.

When the Clinchfield was completed in 1915, Dennis hired Carter's brother-in-law, J. Fred Johnson, as a one-man chamber of commerce for the new town of Kingsport. Johnson was a big man—gregarious, generous, a self-appointed protector of the public morals, and driven by an obsession to create a large, important industrial city on the banks of the Holston River. By this time Carter was no longer involved in the Clinchfield, nor in the new town of Kingsport. It was up to Dennis, himself, to build the city. With the railroad as its centerpiece, Dennis set Johnson to work wooing new industry into Kingsport.

Dozens of retail businesses opened in Kingsport to serve workers. J. Fred Johnson's "Big Store," located on the corner of Main and Shelby Streets (near Center), sold everything from teaspoons to coffins and boasted they could supply the needs of a person "from birth to the grave." Doctors and lawyers moved into Kingsport. Restaurants opened for business.

Dennis insisted that town growth be regulated. He hired John Nolen of Cambridge, Massachusetts, to draw up a plan for a new city of 50,000. In spite of efforts to control growth, however, new people streamed into Kingsport faster than housing could be built to accommodate them. By September 1916, bustling, boomtown-like Kingsport was a lucrative stop for a traveling circus. Men worked all day in factories and stores and had much leisure time on their hands at night and on weekends. Furthermore, money was plentiful, and Kingsport residents were willing to spend it for entertainment.

Sparks World Famous Shows pulled into Kingsport early Tuesday morning. As usual a crowd of boys and young men was on hand at the siding to welcome the circus folk and beg for jobs.

With the help of the elephants, the wagons were unloaded by daybreak, and the big top was well on its way to being raised to full height. Sparks' newest employee, Red Eldridge, elephant stick in hand, led Shadrack, a big Indian elephant, to a stake and waiting chain. Like all Sparks' elephants, Shadrack, about fifteen years old, was a female. Mary, her work done for the morning, was chained next to Shadrack. The other three Sparks elephants were likewise chained to their stakes, and all were soon happily eating hay.

The quintet of pachyderms struck imposing silhouettes against the blood-red streak of morning sky. Clouds of vapor rose from their warm bodies and hot breath. "Red sky at morning, sailor's warning," said a burly roustabout as he walked up to Red. "Red sky at night, sailor's delight."

Red smiled shyly. He was impressed that a person so rough-looking could sound so much like a poet.

The burly roustabout looked up at the sky. "Might rain. Don't think we'll get anything before night, though. At least rain won't come to spoil the parade."

"Ever have a parade in the rain?" Red asked.

"Yeah. Rain doesn't stop it. People come anyway."

"What about the animals getting wet?"

"Don't bother them none. Ain't lost one yet 'cause they got sick. They hold up better than we do." Then the roustabout looked at Red. "Hear the boss says you're doin' a pretty fair job. Says you caught on real quick."

"Thanks," Red replied.

The roustabout eyed Shadrack and Mary. Mary threw a trunkful of hay over her back. In midair the hay exploded into a cloud of stems and dust. "Seems to me them elephants could pull them stakes out of the ground any time they wanted to," he observed. "They're so strong they don't have to stay tied down if they don't want to."

"They must like us," Red answered hopefully.

"Don't reckon so; at least, not very much. I saw one of John Robinson's elephants get loose one time and go berserk. Damn near killed a bunch of people before they finally stopped it."

"What happened?" Red asked.

"They sold it to another circus."

"The elephant?"

"Yeah. When a circus elephant causes trouble, it ain't no good to that show anymore because people are afraid of it. Then the owners sell the beast to another show, and the new owners give it a different name. It's like a brand new animal. If it causes trouble with that show, the owners sell it again—over and over."

The roustabout scratched the two-day-old gray and black stubble on his face with his the back of his forefinger and studied Mary through squinty eyes. "Take that one over there," he continued. "I heard she's been sold a couple of times. They say she's killed a couple of people."

Red was surprised. He had understood that Mary was a gentle and predictable animal, in spite of his uneasy feeling about her. Just then the head trainer walked up with three eager young boys in tow. "Red," he said, "I got some workers for you."

Red smiled condescendingly. When he was a boy he had been in their shoes, hoping for work in exchange for free tickets to a show. He had been in awe of the expert animal trainer that had put him to work. Now he was the employer as well as the "expert." That made him feel important. The trainer and roustabout left, and Red showed the boys the buckets and told them where to fetch water.

"Now don't get too close to them elephants," he advised, pointing to Mary. "See that one?" he told the wide-eyed youths. "She's killed a dozen men. She killed her trainer last week up in Roanoke."

The boys backed off a bit. Red smiled. Sure he had lied to them—just a little lie—but there was no harm in exaggerating a bit so the boys would be more careful. He didn't want their blood on his hands.

As Charlie Sparks had predicted, Kingsport was a lucrative stop for the circus. The matinee crowd overflowed the bleachers, and the evening's performance promised to be even more profitable than the one in the afternoon. If the circus had not been scheduled to be in Erwin the next morning, Sparks would have considered remaining in Kingsport another day.

After the performance, the elephant trainers were scheduled to walk their charges a half mile up Center Street to a pond where the elephants would be able to drink their fill and wade around in the water to their hearts' content. Elephants, like children, love to splash in water. Eldridge was especially happy because he would finally get to ride Mary, the star of the show. The ponderous march to the watering hole was bound to attract gawkers; and, sure enough, at first sight of the elephants, a crowd of onlookers assembled along Center Street. Among them was 19-year-old William Coleman.

The sky was just beginning to overcast when the parade of five elephants began making their way up Center Street. Coleman remembered later that each of the beasts bore a rider, and each rider held an elephant stick to keep the elephants under control. Center Street, surfaced with hard-packed dirt, was a wide thoroughfare that sported a big drainage ditch running down the middle. Buildings were sparse along the route. Instead there were the open fields spotted with tents (which served as temporary dwellings for newly-arrived Kingsport residents). In fact, on one stretch of the road, there was only one building—the ramshackle blacksmith shop of 65-year-old Hench Cox.

Cox had not been to the circus matinee—he was too busy. A new town needed the services of a blacksmith badly, and he was far behind in his work. In fact, not even the commotion caused by the approaching elephants made him look up from his glowing forge.

The elephants, each with a trainer on her back, lumbered up Center Street, trunk to tail, with Mary leading the way. Several pigs, munching happily on a watermelon rind, scattered at their approach. The rind attracted the attention of Mary, who paused momentarily. Anxious to keep the animals moving, Eldridge prodded Mary with his elephant stick. Mary shook a little and snorted.

Once again, Mary reached for the rind with her trunk. The elephants behind her stopped, causing a roadblock. Some people in the crowd began laughing at the inability of the big elephant's trainer to make her obey. Anxious not to hold up the line any longer, and getting a little embarrassed at his lack of control, the impatient Eldridge whacked Mary sharply on the side of her head with his stick. Suddenly, the whites of Mary eyes flared as she wrapped her trunk around Eldridge's slim body; then she lifted him into the air. The crowd gasped.

Mary flung Eldridge through the side of a wooden soft drink stand. There was the sickening crunch of wood and human bones. Then the elephant calmly walked over to where Eldridge was lying, placed her foot over his head and squashed it like a ripe melon. Coleman said later he did not know whether Eldridge was already dead when Mary crushed his skull.

Women screamed, and onlookers scattered into the fields hoping to escape the mad elephant's wrath. The screams and shouting caused blacksmith Hench Cox to charge from his blacksmith shop. In his hand he brandished a 32-20 pistol. He saw Eldridge's mangled body on the ground, his head smashed to a bloody pulp. Big Mary was slowly backing away. The other elephants were loudly trumpeting, adding their noisy contribution to the screaming of onlookers. The trainers on the elephants behind Mary leaped to the ground. Some ran over to Eldridge, while others tried valiantly to keep their excited animals under control.

People were running in all directions trying to escape. Cox naturally assumed one of the elephants had gone berserk, and since Mary was the closest to Eldridge, he fired five times at her. Mary groaned and shook as the bullets struck, but they did not penetrate her tough hide.

Some people in the crowd, including William Coleman, stood their ground, though staying well outside the reach of Mary's trunk. A couple of roustabouts rushed to Mary's side and tried to calm her down. Seeing that the elephant was standing its ground and not attacking anyone else, the crowd began to reassemble. The sight of Eldridge's bloody body on the ground sickened some of them. Suddenly, they began chanting, "Kill the elephant. Let's kill him."

Cox ran back inside his blacksmith shop to reload. The other trainers tried to keep their charges in control, but all was chaos. Since the parade was only a few hundred feet from the circus grounds when all hell broke loose, Charlie Sparks had heard the commotion and the shots. He mounted the nearest horse and galloped up the road, completely forgetting the natural fear the elephants have of horses. Just before he reached the elephants, he remembered that the sight of a horse might make it even harder to control the elephants. He dismounted at a gallop, falling into the mud. His mount took one look at the elephants in front of him and veered off into a vacant field. Sparks scrambled to his feet and ran toward the elephants and the angry crowd.

The roustabouts had Mary under control, but the crowd continued their chant. Sparks saw Eldridge's twisted body and thought for one horrible moment that it might be one of the good citizens of Kingsport that Mary had killed.

"It's Red, sir," one of the roustabouts said breathlessly, "the new trainer."

Sparks was almost relieved that it was one of his own men who had been trampled. Then he glanced at the crowd—the angry crowd chanting "Kill the elephant." Sparks had to think quickly.

"People, I'd be perfectly willing to kill her, but there's no way. There ain't gun enough in this country that she could be killed. There's no way to kill her." Sparks knew that he was lying. Elephants could be killed very easily—even with a shotgun. All you had to do was to fire into their ear canal. Sparks glanced at Mary, who was swaying back and forth nervously. Then he turned to the nearest roustabout. "Get this bunch back to the circus and be quick about it," he hissed.

Even at this point, Charlie Sparks probably didn't entertain the notion that Mary should be destroyed. He probably knew that Mary had killed before—or at least had a strong suspicion that she had. Otherwise why would another circus be so anxious to rid themselves of such a large animal? He, himself, hated to lose so large an elephant, but "rogue" elephants had been sold to other circuses before, names changed, and then sold again. Yes, Sparks was certain of it. This had not been the first time Mary had killed someone.

The first thing J. Fred Johnson did when he heard that a circus elephant had killed its trainer was to inquire if the man had a family. That was J. Fred's way. He always concerned himself with others. Word returned that the man's name was Red Eldridge and that he had joined the circus in St. Paul. Inquiries to St. Paul revealed that Eldridge was not a native.

Instead, he had drifted into town, worked for the Riverside Hotel, had quit and joined the circus. Reports were that Eldridge was from someplace in the midwest. One of the men working with the circus said that he had known Red for "several years" and told the newspapers that he was from somewhere near Mount Vernon, Indiana.

Big, gregarious J. Fred Johnson decided, in absence of next of kin, to take charge of the funeral and burial arrangements of the mangled elephant trainer. He directed B. G. Nunnelly, manager of The Big Store, to furnish a casket and make arrangements with a local funeral director to prepare the body.

Word of Eldridge's violent death spread quickly throughout upper East Tennessee. In a few hours, Mayor S. E. Miller of Johnson City was aware of the incident and decided, along with his chief of police, that no murderous elephant would ever set foot in his town. Sparks World Famous Shows was scheduled to play Johnson City on September 14, two days hence. To compound Sparks' problem, the mayor of Rogersville made a similar decision, preventing the circus from setting up in that town on the 15th.

Word of Mary's ban in Johnson City and Rogersville got back to Charlie Sparks, and he had to make a decision. He tried to talk to his publicist, John Heron, but found him in the middle of an interview with a reporter from the Johnson City *Staff*.

"I very much regret the sad and untimely death of Red," Heron said to the reporter. "We cannot account for Mary's conduct. The affair has cast a gloom over the entire show. We are very sorry."

"Has this kind of thing ever happened before?" the reporter asked.

The little man twitched nervously as he saw Charlie Sparks standing in the doorway. "I have been with the show for three years and have never known the elephant to lose her temper before."

"How long did you know Red."

"I didn't. I didn't even know his name until this sad incident." Then Heron said, "You will have to excuse me. This affair has created many problems for the show."

"Thank you, Mr. Heron," the reporter said. Then he left, looking for someone else to interview. Heron waited until the reporter disappeared before he approached Charlie Sparks.

"John," Sparks said, "we've been banned from Johnson City and Rogersville. According to my sources the circus can play the dates, but without Mary."

"News travels fast." Heron observed dryly. "Mary's the star of the show. Without Mary, there won't be much of a performance. She's on all our advertising.'' Then he said as an afterthought, ''What about tonight's show?''

Sparks thought for a moment. ''I guess we'll try to hold it as usual and hope nobody objects. In the meantime, I have to decide what to do with Mary.''

That night in Kingsport, Mary *did perform* with the circus as usual. The big top was filled to overflowing. Clearly, half of Kingsport wanted to see the killer elephant. Mary and the rest of the elephants were calm, the tragic incident of the afternoon apparently forgotten. Charlie Sparks hoped that the whole sad incident would blow over and he would be able to play both Johnson City and Rogersville *with Mary*. The season was nearly over, and the company would soon take up winter quarters. By next season everyone would have probably forgotten about Mary's behavior.

Johnson City's Mayor Miller determined, however, that the incident would not be forgotten. Already he was talking to the authorities, trying to find a way to force someone to destroy the elephant. His sensibilities had been offended, and they demanded revenge on the killer.

The next day, when the newspapers hit the streets with their accounts of the incident in Kingsport, more fuel was added to the fire. The case arguing for Mary's destruction was growing. Authorities were uneasy about an outraged public's demand for Mary's destruction.

A heavy rain began to fall as the circus finished packing from its stint in Kingsport. Once again, a Clinchfield engine backed up to Sparks' circus train and coupled on. Then the train slowly began moving southeastward as sheets of cold, driving rain pounded down on already dampened spirits. A troubled Charlie Sparks was wrestling with an agonizing decision that he did not want to make. Sleep would not find him for the rest of the night.

Wednesday, September 13, 1916

On the last day of Mary's life, it was business as usual. Early in the morning Sparks' circus train pulled into the little railroad town of Erwin and backed into a convenient siding. An all-night soaking rain had turned the ground into a sticky quagmire. By daybreak most of the heavy rain had stopped, but a fine drizzle continued. Mist partially obscured the Unaka Mountains which edged the east end of town.

Erwin, like Kingsport, was a rough and ready town in those days, growing by leaps and bounds. The Cincinnati, Clinchfield and Ohio

Railroad chose the town to locate new repair facilities; and in only one year the town's population had ballooned to nearly 2,000 people, with more arriving every day.

By 6:30 Sparks' elephants, including Mary, were led from the train and were slogging through the mire, marching steadily toward the end of a long row of flatcars that brought up the rear of the train. A steel run led from the end of the last flatcar. The runway provided a sturdy ramp for the unloading of circus wagons. Roustabouts pushed the first wagon to the end of the flatcar, and Mary stepped between the tracks of the steel run.

"Ho! Mary!" the head trainer snapped, brandishing his elephant stick with the hook on the end. "Mary! Ho!"

Mary sighed heavily, lowered her head and allowed her flat forehead to contact the front of the gaily-colored wagon.

"Ho!"

The roustabouts pushed the wagon onto the steel runway, and, almost instantly, gravity took charge. Mary braced herself on her stubby legs and pushed forward to impede the downward journey of the wagon.

"Ho!" the trainer said.

The roustabouts had already pushed the second red and yellow wagon into place on the ramp by the time Mary eased the first one to the ground. The earth was soft, and the spoked wheel sunk into the soft earth just above the rim, squeezing out a tiny pond of muddy water from the turf on either side of the iron tire.

"Ho, Mary!" the trainer snapped, tapping her gently on the leg with his hooked stick. Mary raised her head and took a few ponderous steps backward. A two-horse team of grays appeared and hitched to the wagon's singletree. Mary watched the horses warily. She had worked with horses before, but she, like most elephants, considered horses her natural enemy.

(The shout of "Hold your horses, here come the elephants," carried a warning of danger to all who heard it.)

The grays were hitched, the driver climbed into the driver's box, and the heavy wagon lumbered off toward the vacant city lot where the circus would take up temporary residence. The journey barely began when the wagon ran into a soft spot and sunk up to its right wheel axle. With the axle buried, the wagon would require more than the tug of a team of powerful horses to pull her loose.

"Dang!" Mary's trainer muttered.

"Hey!" the teamster shouted from the crazily slanted driver's box. "I need help."

"I don't doubt you do," Mary's trainer yelled back sarcastically. "Why don't you look where you're a-goin'?"

"Just get that beast workin'," the driver shouted. "We've got a lot to do around here this mornin'."

Mary's trainer poked his stick into Mary's shoulder, just enough to prod her in the direction of the disabled wagon. Meanwhile, amused roustabouts on top of the flatcar leaned against the second wagon and prepared to watch Mary do her stuff.

"Ho! Mary! Yo!" the trainer said, tapping the end of the mired wagon with the elephant stick.

For a moment Mary was confused as to what she was required to do. She stood in one place, swaying gently.

"Ho, Mary," the trainer said, tapping the end of the wagon again. Mary lowered her head and butted against the end of the wagon. The trainer tapped her gently with his stick. "Push, girl."

Mary began to shove, and the wagon responded instantly. She then let up the pressure, and the wagon rolled back into the mire. Mary, thinking her job finished, stepped back with a snort.

"Whoa," the trainer said, stepping aside smartly before the five-ton animal trod on his foot. Then he craned his neck so he could see around the side of the wagon. He shouted to the teamster. "Hey, buddy! Your mules need to pull too."

One of the other elephants standing by trumpeted as if in agreement. Mary snorted, and the roustabouts on the flatcar began to laugh.

The disgusted wagon driver grunted, turned toward his horses and snapped the reins. "Haa! Heeeyyyaaaa!" The horses sprung into action, straining against the heavy weight behind them. "Heeyyyaaaa!"

In an instant, with Mary's help, the wagon was free and on its way toward the vacant field, the driver mumbling to himself about uppity elephant trainers.

On the morning of September 13, the Johnson City *Staff* reached Kingsport with the story about Eldridge's murder. Everyone in town was talking about it. Mayor Miller and the chief of police stuck to their guns. Sparks World Famous Shows could play Johnson City, but *not* with Mary. The city fathers of Rogersville had issued a similar ultimatum. In Kingsport, Eldridge's broken body had been embalmed under J. Fred Johnson's orders, then sent to St. Paul for burial. And citizen unrest over the murder in Kingsport was growing.

The problem for most people was that Eldridge's beastly killer *was still alive*. Citizens were up in arms and determined to do something about the animal so she would never kill again. So many stories had been written in newspapers, and Mary was now so notorious, that it would be nearly impossible for Charlie Sparks to sell Mary to another circus. Neither could he afford to pass up play dates in Johnson City or Rogersville.

By mid-morning, most people in Erwin also knew that Mary had killed a man in Kingsport the day before, but they had been more philosophical about it. At least there were no general uprisings there, and the city fathers were not issuing ultimatums like thunderbolts. While the circus was being set up in Erwin, Charlie Sparks sat in his railroad car, still trying to make a decision about Mary.

Unsettling questions nagged him. Would he be personally held responsible for Eldridge's death? Rumors spread that Mary had killed before—as many as 15 men, according to some stories. Furthermore, word also spread that Sparks, himself, had been fully aware of Mary's murderous tendencies. That part of the rumor was partially true. When he bought Mary for his show, he only suspected that the elephant had a reputation as a killer. He took a chance on her because he believed she might have mellowed with age. Besides, Mary—being female—was not as unpredictable as some of the more notorious male bulls of early traveling circuses.

Nearly everyone connected with the circus knew about the reputations surrounding Hannibal, Romeo, Columbus and Bolivar—all rogue elephants who performed in circuses during the nineteenth century. Hannibal, alone, was said to have killed seven persons. Hannibal, however, was a male apparently crazed by musth. When it came to the behavior of elephants, this made a big difference.

The public knew nothing of elephant physiology or musth. To them, an elephant was an elephant and you couldn't have a circus without one. The public could not have cared less if an elephant was male or female. Elephants were as intrinsic to the big top as acrobats and clowns.

Charlie Sparks also had to consider Mary's material worth. Elephants didn't come cheap. Mary was worth about $8,000—a small fortune in 1916. The destruction of Mary would cause Sparks a financial setback—but so would all those cancelled play dates.

Sparks had also heard rumors that the State of Tennessee was getting in on the act and was going to order the elephant destroyed. Furthermore, he had heard that a vigilante committee from Kingsport was on its way to Erwin, armed with a relic Civil War cannon, intending to kill Mary themselves. After Mary had killed Eldridge in Kingsport, Sparks had told the angry mob there wasn't a gun big enough in

Tennessee to destroy her. Well, clearly, the good citizens of Kingsport had found themselves a gun that they believed could do the job. Sparks' dark thoughts were interrupted by a knock on the door. Who was that—the sheriff? "Come in," Sparks said nervously.

The door opened and in walked publicist John Heron. He slumped down in the chair opposite Charlie Sparks.

"How's the unloading going?" Sparks asked.

"OK, I guess."

"And Mary?"

"She's fine, no problem."

Charlie nearly laughed out loud. "No problem?"

Heron clarified himself. "With her behavior, I mean. Have you figured out what you're going to do about her yet?"

"No," Sparks replied. "You've heard the rumors, of course?"

"About the lynch mob and the cannon they're bringing down from Kingsport?"

"And others—they're buzzing around like flies at the swimming hole." Sparks thought for a moment, then he said: "You know we're going to have to do something. In the public interest, I mean."

"Destroy her."

"I think so," Sparks replied sadly. "I don't see any other way out. I don't think we can sell her to another show. And if we keep her we may lose important play dates. Johnson City and Rogersville have already declared that Mary cannot come into their towns."

"By the way," Heron said with a thin smile. "Did you know that we tried to electrocute Mary back in Kingsport yesterday?"

Charlie Sparks' eyebrows nearly flew off his face in surprise. "We did?"

"Yep. According to one person I talked to this morning, he said he heard we attached 44,000 volts to Mary and threw the switch. The fellow said she shook a little bit, but the electricity didn't faze her at all."

Sparks smiled weakly.

Heron leaned back in his chair, drew a cigarette out of a crumpled pack, and lit it. He exhaled and let the blue smoke lazily encircle his head for a moment. Then he said, "I was talking to one of the Clinchfield engineers a few minutes ago. He asked what we were going to do about Mary. I said I didn't know. Then he asked whether we had considered killing her and I said we had. He made a suggestion."

"What was it?" Sparks asked.

"Well..." Heron began, "you're not going to like this. He suggested that we take her down to the railroad yards, tie a chain around her neck and to one engine and one around her body and to another engine. Then the two engines would pull apart and tear her head off.''

"Damn!"

"I know," Heron answered. "I found it rather disgusting, myself. I told him that Mary wasn't just another piece of flesh. I said there were a lot of circus folks who thought highly of the animal. Then the helpful fellow made another suggestion.''

"I shudder to ask what it was.''

Heron smiled benignly. "He says the railroad has a big 100-ton derrick car unloading lumber in Johnson City. He thinks the railroad would bring the car back to the yards so that we could hang Mary from it.''

"Like a gallows?''

"Yeah. That's what the fellow said.''

What a novel idea, Sparks thought sadly. That would make one hell of an encore for Mary.

"Personally I fancy the idea," Heron continued, nonplussed. "Newspapers will cover the story and there will be a lot of free publicity. I mean if we have to kill her, let's do it with style. That way our dissenting friends in Johnson City and Rogersville will have not the slightest doubt in their vengeful heads that Mary is *really* dead. Surely, there would be plenty of eyewitnesses to attest to the fact. And I think hanging would be more humane than any of the other suggestions that I've heard this morning.''

Charlie Sparks stood up, walked to a window, and looked out onto the circus grounds. In the distance, the elephants were peacefully munching hay. Without turning back to Heron he said, "When do we do it?''

"Today," Heron replied. "I suggest right after the matinee.''

"And you say the railroad will cooperate?''

"I think so. At least, the engineer I talked to thought they would.''

Charlie Sparks sighed heavily. "Then I'll leave it to you. You make all the arrangements.'' Then Sparks slowly turned and Heron saw his eyes were rimmed with red. "God, John. I hope we're doing the right thing!''

Erwin, the county seat of Unicoi County, had a checkered history— a history of sometimes uncertain progress, of near hits and misses. In fact the name *Erwin*, itself, was a mistake.

Originally, the name of the town was to be *Ervin* in honor of David Ervin, who had donated 15 acres of the land to Unicoi County. Ervin was in the mercantile business with Frank Toney. The pair also owned a store in Limestone Cove. The United States Post Office erred in recording the name and called the town Erwin. The error was never corrected.

The town grew slowly at first. In 1900, the population of the Fifth Judicial District of Unicoi County, which included Erwin, stood at 798. The Holston Land Company bought land in the town, laid out the streets, and sold lots. Company president R. S. Chevis dreamed of Erwin as a planned community. In 1909 the Clinchfield Railroad decided to move its repair facilities to Erwin. The population boomed. A year later the population mushroomed to 1149 in Erwin alone. This was too much for David Ervin, the original benefactor. He hated crowds. Ervin sold most of his land in town to the Holston Land Company for railroad shops. Then he picked up bag and baggage and removed himself to neighboring Washington County.

Hank S. Johnson, whose father was a car repairman on the Clinchfield, remembered a "western" flavor in Erwin in those days when the rush began. "The town was sprouting like a boy growing too fast for his own britches."

Erwin had reached the gangly stage in 1916. Streets were ankle-deep with yellow mud. Sidewalks were actually boardwalks. Residents made their own soap and hand-dug their own wells. What Erwinites could not make for themselves, the general store of Tucker and Toney provided. There was also a hotel in town, as well as a couple of small restaurants. The Holston Land Company planned for a final population in Erwin of 30,000 people, and, for a while, it looked like the goal was attainable. By September 1916, the town had an estimated 2,000 residents.

During the Wednesday afternoon matinee, Mary was staked out behind the main tent, near the entrance to Dr. Harvey's office. Both front feet were firmly chained to stout wooden stakes pounded deep into the wet ground. Mary spent the day swaying back and forth, far more than she usually did. Obviously she was very nervous. In light of her uncertain mood, her trainer thought that chaining both feet might be wise.

Inside the tent the show proceeded normally, but Mary sensed something was wrong. She was chained in back of the tent and was not performing. By now the people who worked for the circus, as well as most of the town, knew Mary was to be hung after the matinee. The roustabouts and everyone else she came in contact with suddenly treated her differently. Although she could not have known the plans for the hanging, the behavioral change of the humans around her must have been unsettling to the animal.

Then Mary was aware of a human figure standing close by—someone she didn't recognize. Wade Ambrose, a former Clinchfield Railroad employee, was loitering outside the circus tent, saw the elephant, and fearlessly approached. Mary, curious, reached out with her trunk, and Ambrose thought that she was begging for food. Unfortunately, he had nothing on hand—not even a peanut.

The elephant snorted and reached out a second time, straining at her bonds. Her trunk was now only inches away from Ambrose. Suddenly someone grabbed Ambrose and whirled him around.

"You danged fool," a big circus roustabout growled.

"What's the matter?" Ambrose said innocently. "What did I do?"

"That elephant was trying to get a-hold of you. She's already killed two men, and she was trying to get a-hold of you!"

Ambrose's eyes widened. Was this *the killer elephant* authorities were preparing to lynch for murder? Instantly, Ambrose moved back out of her reach—way back!

In the meantime, inside the circus tent, the last act occupied the spotlight. The show was winding down to its conclusion.

———

Sixteen-year-old Guard Banner, a car man for the Clinchfield Railroad, was scraping dirt and grime from underneath a rusty hopper when he heard "Ol' Fourteen Hundred" steam into the yard. The 100-ton derrick car was back early. Banner thought she was still unloading lumber in Johnson City.

Fourteen Hundred steamed onto a siding near the turntable and screeched to a halt. Banner crawled out from under the hopper as Bud Jones, the acting fireman, jumped down off the engine.

"What you doin' back so soon?" Banner asked him.

"Search me," Jones replied. "We got an urgent call to come to the yard."

A hiss and a white cloud of steam escaped from the boiler, momentarily obscuring Jones. "You seen Sam any place?"

"No," Banner answered. "I've been under that hopper most of the day."

Jones nodded and walked off in search of Sam Bondurant, the derrick wreck master. Then "One-Eyed" Sam Harvey, the assistant derrick engineer, emerged from the tiny metal engine cab. "Where's Jeff?" Guard asked, referring to Jeff Stultz, the regular engineer.

"Hello, Guard. Reckon he went off to Virginia to visit relatives. You seen Sam Bondurant around?"

"Nope," Banner answered.

"Wish I knew why we was called back so quick." Then Harvey's one good eye fell on Banner. "You got any idea what all this is about?"

"Not me. I was as surprised to see you fellers as you were to come back."

Bud Jones returned with Sam Bondurant. "Sam," he called, "fire up the boiler. We got us an elephant to hang."

Of course Harvey thought he was joking. "Ain't no joke," Bondurant said. "Them circus people need an elephant hung. It killed a feller over in Kingsport."

The curious Banner eased in closer so he could hear what the three men were saying.

"I ain't gettin' near that thing," Sam Harvey declared.

Bondurant smiled. "Don't worry none, Sam. Them circus people are going to slip that chain around his neck. They know what they're a-doin'. All you have to do is pull the switch."

"I can do that all right. When?"

"Right after the matinee."

When the afternoon matinee ended, some of the crowd expressed displeasure that Mary, the killer elephant, had not performed in the show. However, it did not take long for word to spread that the circus planned to hang the elephant in the Clinchfield Railroad yards right after the performance. Best of all, the spectacle would be free.

Shortly before 4 p.m., a crowd of onlookers began assembling at the Clinchfield Railroad yard near the turntable and powerhouse. Those attending the circus matinee walked from the tent, located between Gay and Tucker Streets, northwest down Nolichucky Avenue, rounded the new red brick Clinchfield passenger station, and spilled across the track-strewn yard to the roundhouse. Latecomers streamed across the wooden bridges that spanned the Nolichucky River and North Indian Creek, or they made their way up Main Street or Jonesborough Highway. The curious arrived in wagons, on horse, afoot and even by car.

Wade Ambrose reached the yard before most of the others and found a vantage point atop a handy boxcar. Guard Banner settled on the iron cowcatcher of a locomotive parked about 50 feet from the turntable, directly across from Ol' Fourteen Hundred. Guard's father, Henry, also an employee of the Clinchfield, was somewhere in the gathering crowd, but Guard couldn't spot him.

The pretty young daughter of the wreck car foreman Sam Bondurant had found a ringside seat on top of another boxcar. W. B. Carr and

F. W. Talley, Clinchfield machine shop employees, dropped what they were doing to see the elephant hung. They shared the cowcatcher with young Guard Banner.

Ten-year-old Lonnie Bailey, the son of Clinchfield welder Dave Bailey, stood in a boisterous crowd of excited, noisy schoolboys. Lonnie had not attended the circus matinee that afternoon, but he had walked all the way from his house on Third Street to witness the hanging. His mother, Lizzie, had told him to go ahead without her and that she would be along directly. She had also warned him to be careful.

Back at the circus, the main tent cleared quickly. Patrons all wanted a good seat for the hanging, so they hurried out as soon as the show was over. Circus employees, too, wanted to be there. Clowns hastily smeared white cold cream on their faces to remove white greasepaint makeup. Agile acrobats changed from brightly-colored circus outfits into drab street clothes. Henri Mordette (the acrobat who "walked" on his head) changed into his street clothes while his friend, Captain Tiebor, caged his "educated sea lions."

Mary's trainer waited patiently until everyone was ready. When Mary marched to the scaffold, circus folk would accompany her. Nearly every employee wanted to be on hand for Mary's execution; they were determined to pay last respects. Mary wasn't just another circus elephant to them—she was the star of the show.

One acrobat, a woman who had ridden Mary in hundreds of circus parades and had worked with her often in the ring, walked briskly from the circus grounds and into town. When she passed someone, she hid her tear-streaked face. She loved Mary and could not bear to see her destroyed. The woman disappeared into a shabby room at one of the town's hotels, locked the door behind her and began to sob uncontrollably.

In the meantime, the head animal trainer for Sparks World Famous Shows checked on Mary and prepared her for her last walk. The elephant was visibly nervous, and the trainer decided it would be dangerous to lead Mary to the Clinchfield yards alone. She had been chained all during the matinee and was fully aware that a performance was going on without her. One of the roustabouts told him that she had even tried to kill another person (Ambrose).

The trainer decided he would take the entire herd of elephants on Mary's last walk. He hoped the company of other elephants would have a calming effect. Assistants brought up the rest of the herd, and with the help of roustabouts, the trainer loosed Mary's bonds.

Excited beyond words, 16-year-old Guard Banner stood on the cowcatcher of the Clinchfield engine, craning his neck to see the crowd of 2,500 people assembled in the railroad yards. Every engine, every boxcar, every piece of rolling stock was overflowing with spectators. A tall coal tipple was literally black with people hanging onto every available space.

Young Banner spotted 49-year-old Jim Coffey, a blind banjo picker with whom he had hunted on occasion. Banner had worked as a delivery man for Liberty Lumber Company before he signed on to work for the Clinchfield. One day he delivered a load of weatherboard to Coffey's frame house outside Erwin. Coffey accepted the shipment, paid for the siding in cash, then promptly installed the siding himself, without help from anyone. Coffey's independence from his blindness didn't surprise Banner. There was another occasion when Coffey dramatically proved his ability to "see" without eyes.

Henry Banner, Guard's father, took Coffey possum hunting on Buffalo Mountain one Saturday night. The men and dogs split into two groups for the hunt. "Somehow they got runnin' together," Banner remembered 75 years later. "The dogs got to treein' and we got together and everybody got lost. They didn't know where they were. Jim Coffey asked them if there was an oak tree around there. They told him there was and he said to lead him to it.

"He went over to that oak tree, which was probably three feet 'round. He felt around the oak tree. Then he said, 'Go right down there and hit this holler and you'll come out at Indian Creek, a little ways off down the mountain.' You couldn't fool Jim Coffey in the mountains. He'd tell you the way out."

Banner also admired Coffey's skill as a musician, especially at community dances. "Back then, people, they'd have ice cream suppers," Banner remembered, "and just have a good time. Didn't have no drinking going on. It was just a clean get-together. Jim'd play banjo, and people would have a wonderful time. He'd pick for them. He'd do it for free."

Right now, from Guard's vantage point on the engine, Jim Coffey looked like he was in unfamiliar territory. As he walked, he kept bumping into people, or they into him. Finally Coffey decided to stand still and find out what would happen next.

Shortly after 4 o'clock someone shouted, "Here come the elephants." The crowd craned their necks. A procession of five elephants, walking trunk to tail, ambled from the circus grounds onto Nolichucky Avenue, turning South on Tucker Street, then to Main. Miss Bondurant, from

her vantage point atop the boxcar, noticed that the circus people followed the procession in double file—"some looking sad, some crying."

When the procession turned northwest onto Second Street, passing between Liberty Lumber on the right and Crystal Ice and Coal Company on the left, fireman Bud Jones thought something was wrong with the elephants. Mary was acting up—hesitating and bellowing at the top of her voice. The other elephants were joining in noisy accompaniment to Mary's trumpeting. Jones had an eerie feeling that *Mary knew exactly what was going to happen.*

From his vantage point atop the engine, W. B. Carr also noticed the elephant handlers were having difficulty keeping their charges together and moving. Mary continued to trumpet wildly. Then she stopped and squatted on the ground, and the handlers used the other elephants to get Mary up and going again. Carr told Talley that he couldn't help feeling sorry for the condemned elephant.

The lumbering procession crossed three spur tracks which ran across Second Street (the Jonesborough Road). The elephants noticed three sinkholes filled with water to the right and began moving off to the side. The handlers knew that if the herd made their way into those pools, it would be difficult getting them back out again. Fortunately for everyone concerned, the men were able to keep the procession in line, on the road, and moving steadily toward the railroad yard.

From Second Street, the procession turned onto an old dirt road that led to the railroad yards and crossed a muddy little tributary of North Indian Creek. Then they turned southeast toward the roundhouse, passing between the machine shop and powerhouse. The elephants passed waiting Derrick No. 1400, stopping just short of the roundhouse and turntable.

From his position on Ol' Fourteen Hundred, fireman Bud Jones, like Guard Banner, noticed the large number of people on the coal tipple. He hoped the tower could withstand the weight. He, too, estimated the crowd at about 3,000 people—more folks than actually lived in Erwin. Where on earth had they all come from? He was also amazed at the size of an elephant, now that he saw one up close.

Dave Bailey, on duty in the Clinchfield shops, was fixing a broken engine post with an acetylene torch when curiosity finally drew him outside to see what was going on. In fact, all Clinchfield employees, still at work, left their posts to watch the hanging. Well-scrubbed faces— male and female—peered from the windows of the brand new office building the Clinchfield had built the year before.

About 500 feet farther down the track, railroad laborers and circus roustabouts had dug a hole for Mary's body after the hanging. Bud Jones said the hole was as "big as a barn".

Roustabouts quickly chained Mary's leg to the rail. Mary shook, swayed and trumpeted. Handlers began leading the other animals away so they could not see their companion being hung. Mary panicked and tried to pull loose, but she was securely fastened to the rail.

The crowd in the yard murmured expectantly. Puddles dotted the ground from the heavy rain. A sticky combination of mud, cinders, oil and coal dust clung to leather shoes like cement. An atmosphere of gloom shrouded the scene. There was a feeling of uncertainty as well as anticipation. Certainly the mood was not festive—rather it was somber and subdued. Mary clearly sensed something was wrong. Her natural back-and-forth swaying gained a nervous edge. The extra adrenaline coursing through her body might give her enough strength to pull loose—then she would be impossible to control. There could be another killer rampage.

While they waited, rumors continued to circulate through the crowd that Mary had killed before, and if she got loose, she would run through the crowd and murder all of them. She was an outlaw rogue who lashed out suddenly, seized a hapless victim in her trunk, and dashed the body to the ground in a murderous rage. She had also recently acquired a nickname suitable to her reputation—"Murderous Mary." Had Mary really killed up to 20 men before, as some people were now saying? Certainly, she had killed a man in Kingsport. There were eyewitnesses. A full account had been published in the newspapers.

One local minister declared that Mary was demon-possessed. Exorcise the demon, he advised, and the animal would be fine. If Charlie Sparks had been a religious man, he would have given the minister leave to proceed with the exorcism.

Elephants are among the most intelligent and perceptive of mammals. From Mary's point of view, there were crowds of people standing around, but no tent. This was no performance in the sense that Mary understood it. Her familiar props were absent. No one had placed the huge ornate gold-braided blanket on her back or the fancy halter on her head. Mary also sensed a change in her handlers. Their usual firm patience in dealing with the elephant was absent, replaced with a strong sense of urgency. Mary had found herself in a railroad yard—a familiar spot for Mary. She might be prepared to work, but where were the gaily-colored wagons to push up the steel incline, onto the flatcars?

As her companions trudged back to the circus grounds without her, Mary grew even more nervous. Elephants are social creatures, and the presence of others of their kind has a pacifying effect. Mary shook violently when she discovered she was abandoned. Little clouds of straw dust rose from her dark gray hide. Her ridiculously small eyes, whites now prevalent, watched in terror as her companions, walking trunk to tail, disappeared behind the powerhouse.

Suddenly, there was more trumpeting. From atop the boxcar, Ambrose could see the other elephants had stopped and were trying to reverse their direction. Handlers scurried around, trying to turn their charges back toward town. Obviously, the other elephants did not want to leave Mary. The handlers continued to work with the elephants and finally got them turned around again. According to Ambrose, no one dared to do anything to Mary until the other elephants were well on their way back to town and out of sight.

Ambling down Second Street, the returning elephants spied the water-filled sinkholes that lay just off the dirt road. This time there was little the handlers could do to prevent their charges from leaving the road. A moment later all four elephants were in the water, happily splashing away. It was fortunate that, from the sinkholes, the elephants could not see the deed being done to their leader.

Sam Harvey and Bud Jones were joined by sixteen-year-old Mont Lilly and two other derrick car crewmen, as well as a couple of burly roustabouts from the circus. A ⅞-inch chain dangled from the derrick boom. One of the roustabouts threw the end of the chain around Mary's neck and fitted the end through a steel ring. Mary started to bolt, and the other men scrambled to safety. Harvey dove into his control cab to get out of the way. The crowd of 3,000 people waited breathlessly. Nothing happened for a long moment, then the nervous Sam Harvey threw the stick forward, and the winch began to squeal.

Slowly, the powerful derrick motor began reeling in the chain. In a moment, the chain began to tighten around Mary's neck, slipping taut through the ring. Mary's head was lifted. Her wind was being cut off. Her front feet left the ground. Mary struggled. In a moment, her hind legs lifted and began to wiggle back and forth, one leg at a time, as if in slow motion. Soon she dangled five or six feet above the muddy ground of the railroad yard.

Suddenly, there came a report like a rifle crack and ricochet, and Mary fell heavily on her rump with a sickening crunch. The cable had snapped. The killer elephant was loose. Immediately, everyone started to run. Bud Jones climbed the crane tower in a panic. Ten-year-old Lonnie Bailey took off and ran into a briar patch, scratching himself badly.

Blind Jim Coffey sensed the panic of the crowd; he had heard the thud when Mary hit the ground. He began running like everyone else. His sixth sense—that had served him so faithfully before—failed him, and he ran headlong into an equally panicked onlooker. Both were knocked to the ground and nearly trampled by the human stampede running over them. They sprung to their feet, and the man yelled at Coffey, "What's the matter, can't you see?"

"Hell no," Coffey screamed back. "I ain't seen a lick in 20 years. I just come down to watch 'em hang the elephant."

Meanwhile, Mary sat on her haunches like a big jack rabbit; she had broken her hip in the fall. The crowd needn't have run, because Mary wasn't going anywhere. One of the roustabouts ran up her back like he was climbing a small hill and attached a heavier chain. The crowd soon saw they had nothing to fear and began slowly drifting back to the scene.

Sam Harvey, once again, put his winch into motion. Once again the chain tightened, and once again Mary was slowly lifted into the air. Gravely injured by her fall, she fought less this time around. The chain held, and a few minutes later Mary fell limp. She was dead.

Elizabeth Bailey was not keen on actually joining the rest of the crowd at the Clinchfield yard to watch the elephant hung, because she feared a beast so large. But, like most people in Erwin, she was curious. She walked down from her house on Third Street to Main, turned left and walked another block to the corner of Second Street. That, she figured, was far enough. Standing on the corner between Liberty Lumber and Crystal Ice and Coal, she looked across the field.

By the time she arrived, the elephant was hanging from the derrick, slowly twisting on the cable around its neck. The only chore remaining was to drop the animal into its grave and shovel the dirt in over her.

There was nothing for spectators left to see, and they began to disperse. A photograph of the grisly scene was snapped to record the event for posterity. T. K. Broyles, a Clinchfield employee, was alleged to have made the famous photograph of Mary hanging from the makeshift gallows, her trunk extended at an abnormal angle. Later the photograph was proclaimed a fake by *Argosy* Magazine.

A few days after the hanging, and after Mary was buried, the Associated Press was said to have approached the Clinchfield Railroad with an odd proposition. They would exhume the body, hoist the dead elephant on the crane again, and take pictures of their own. Understandably, Clinchfield management refused.

The excitement of Mary's hanging had scarcely abated when Sparks presented the evening show in Erwin. An estimated two thousand people packed the big tent in Erwin to watch the farewell performance of the circus. Nearly all the circus patrons that night had attended the lynching of Mary that afternoon.

Ever since the hanging, the remaining four elephants had been nervous, swaying back and forth, throwing small clumps of hay over their backs. Trainers noticed the elephants were not responding to commands as quickly as before. Although the elephants had not actually seen the hanging itself, all were noticeably affected by the mysterious absence of Mary. The keepers were as nervous as their elephants and were not taking as many liberties with them as before. Raw tension and anticipation surrounded the entire evening's performance.

Captain Tiebor performed with his trained seals under the tent. Rubber balls flew through the air from seal to seal. Only moments before, the animals had been tossing firebrands back and forth. In the meantime, one of the clowns made his way through the stands, shaking hands with the hundreds of children attending the performance. High above the ground, aerialists were swinging from trapeze to trapeze.

Charlie Sparks himself attended the show. He noticed that everything looked the same, except that Mary was absent. The loss of Mary was going to cost Sparks dearly. First, there was Mary's monetary value—$8,000. She was not insured; the circus would have to absorb the loss. Then there were the posters with her picture on them. That would all have to be changed, unless he could buy another large elephant before next spring and call her "Mary." Furthermore there was the loss of ticket sales. Mary was clearly a box office draw, and her passing was going to dig deeply into Charlie Sparks' take. Any way he looked at it, Sparks was faced with a stiff financial loss over the death of "Murderous Mary."

Suddenly he had an idea. All was not lost. Calling three of his roustabouts, he ordered them to take shovels and walk down to the Clinchfield yard. "Dig around where the head is and cut off Mary's tusks," he told them. "They're valuable."

The roustabouts went off on their grisly mission, and Sparks turned back to the show. The elephants were now performing, doing the same stunts they had done for years—but without Mary. The trainers were as plainly nervous as the elephants as they put them through the paces.

When the elephants' performance ended, the trainers led the quartet to the exit. Just as the procession reached the outer rim of the tent, next to the reserved seats, Shadrack broke away from the rest of the herd.

Bellowing at the top of her voice, she blundered beneath the grand-stands and threatened to topple the whole affair. According to an account which appeared September 14, 1916, in the Johnson City *Staff*:

> Someone yelled "The elephants are loose," but this was superfluous as the angry snort had already warned the people, who arose as if a chunk of dynamite had been fired beneath them and broke into a mob, yelling, screaming, fighting their way to the middle of the tent and seeking an exit. Women tumbled over, men were knocked down in the wild scramble, hats were smashed, skirts were torn in the effort to get away. Only the hasty capture of the beast by the keeper saved life. As it was many were painfully bruised, but none seriously.

Do elephants, one of the most intelligent of the earth's four-legged creatures, have a conception of the finality of death? Legend says that, in the jungle, old and sick elephants wander off to a special place where they can die in peace. Did Shadrack fully understand the reason for Mary's absence and seek revenge on the puny creatures who brought death to her leader?

As with so many questions raised by Mary's story, we may never know the answer. All we can reasonably do is to speculate and wonder about that enigma, just a part of a true tale that is literally rife with enigmas.

Afterword

When an elephant belonging to an obscure traveling circus became the central figure in one of the most bizarre executions to ever take place in Tennessee—or anywhere else for that matter—the tale of "Murderous Mary" joined the legends of "the Devil's Looking Glass" and the "Banshee of the Nolichucky River" as an invaluable piece of upper East Tennessee folklore.

In this book, I have attempted to replace folklore and myth with logic, coupled with as many hard facts as I could muster. I will readily admit that some of the situations in this book have been partially fabricated to fill in voids where facts were lacking. But even these diversions from strict fact are based in truth. There is, for example, no solid proof that Charlie Sparks, owner of the circus, had an early-morning conversation with publicist Bill Heron concerning Mary's fate. Circus records do not document any such meeting. But it is reasonably certain that various methods of destroying the elephant were discussed with Sparks on the morning of the execution, including the inhumane solutions mentioned in the mythical conversation. I think this conversation—or one very much like it—could, and probably did, take place.

Through research and careful elimination, I believe I have pieced together a fair reconstruction of the events leading up to and including the execution of "Murderous Mary." All the people mentioned in this story are real—none are fictitious. A number of eyewitnesses to the hanging are still living, and, whenever possible, I interviewed them extensively.

Several other interviews with eyewitnesses were recorded on tape by East Tennessee State University professors Thomas Burton and Ambrose Manning in the late 1960s. The tapes are now on file in the Burton-Manning folklore collection at ETSU. These were also used in researching material for this book.

There have not been any large scale works written on the hanging, so most of my research is based on primary sources. The few articles written in recent years about the elephant are filled with errors and are clearly influenced by the oral tradition. The best is an article by Tom Burton himself, published in the *Tennessee Folklore Society Bulletin* in 1971. Burton's article is based on the interviews he recorded a few years before. Burton, however, only touches on the high points of the story. His treatment of Red Eldridge is perfunctory. This is understandable since information on Eldridge is as hard to find as water on the moon.

No one knows where Eldridge came from, but the general feeling is that he was born and raised in Indiana, moved east when opportunities in the midwest dwindled, and somehow ended up in St. Paul, Virginia. He was clearly a drifter, however, but worked for a short time at the Riverside Hotel. These snippets of conjecture and the few biographical facts in the days before his death are about all we know of this pivotal character in Mary's story.

Most of the people mentioned in this book are dead. "One-Eyed" Sam Harvey, the crane operator who actually hung Mary, died on January 26, 1938, at age 55. Bud Jones, fireman on the crane car, was born in 1888 and died in 1978, about ten years after Burton interviewed him. Mont Lilly died two years earlier than Jones, in 1976, and is buried in Evergreen Cemetery, south of Erwin. The blind banjo picker who was run down by fleeing spectators when the chain broke around Mary's neck died in 1935 and is also buried in Evergreen Cemetery.

Guard Banner, born on November 6, 1899, is still alive at this writing and living just outside Erwin. Hank Johnson, who was in Mexico with the U.S. Army fighting Pancho Villa when Mary was hung, but who provided vivid details about the "boom town" of Erwin, retired from the Clinchfield Railroad in 1956. He is 98 years old and currently lives in Erwin.

On Thursday, September 14, 1916, Sparks World Famous Shows traveled to Johnson City and performed there. The Johnson City *Staff* reported that "The big tent was almost filled to capacity this afternoon and if the applause of the audience is any criterion of the size of the house tonight then the walls of the tent will bulge with pleasure-seeking humanity." The *Staff* continued its story by reminding patrons that Sparks would move on to Rogersville the next day for two more performances. There was no mention of Mary or the hanging in the article. Apparently all had been forgiven—at least in Johnson City and Rogersville.

And what of Mary? Of course, she died on September 13, 1916, and is buried somewhere in the railroad yards at Erwin—fortunately no one knows where. The location of the grave has been lost over the years, and that is just as well. If her life, death, and memory have not been allowed to rest, maybe, at least, we can leave her body in peace.

This is the only photograph known to exist that shows the hanging of Mary the elephant. It was taken by an unknown photographer about 5:00 p.m., September 13, 1916, just before the animal was buried in the Clinchfield Railroad Yards in Erwin. Photographic expert Eddie LeSueur believes the photo was snapped by an amateur photographer, using a Kodak folding camera. Since it was drizzling rain when the photo was taken, the image appears somewhat fuzzy. The original negative no longer exists, and subsequent prints have often been touched up. This print was made from a copy negative. (Photo courtesy of Eddie LeSueur)

A recent photograph of 93-year-old Guard Banner of Erwin, one of the last surviving eyewitnesses to the hanging. Banner was a 16-year-old Clinchfield employee in September 1916. (Photo by Larry Smith/ETSU University Relations)

The crew of Ol' 1400, the Clinchfield Railroad's 100-ton derrick car on which the elephant was hung, poses for a group portrait around 1913. To the left, sitting on the derrick boom, is "One-Eyed" Sam Harvey, the regular fireman, who actually hung the elephant. To the right is the regular derrick operator, Jeff Stultz, who was in Roanoke the day Mary was hung. The unidentified man in the middle may be Sam Bondurant, the derrick car foreman. (Photo courtesy of The Unicoi County Heritage Museum, Erwin)

Bud Jones, in later years, holds a model of "1402", a 200-ton derrick car. Ol' 1400 was a 100-ton car.